LAID OFF AND LOVING IT

LAID OFF AND LOVING IT

How to Survive a Catastrophe

David Tallman

TATE PUBLISHING & *Enterprises*

Published by Tate Publishing & Enterprises, LLC
127 E. Trade Center Terrace | Mustang, Oklahoma 73064 USA
1.888.361.9473 | www.tatepublishing.com

Tate Publishing is committed to excellence in the publishing industry. The company reflects the philosophy established by the founders, based on Psalm 68:11,
"The Lord gave the word and great was the company of those who published it."

Book design copyright © 2010 by Tate Publishing, LLC. All rights reserved.
Cover design by Kristen Verser
Interior design by Stefanie Rane

Published in the United States of America

ISBN: 978-1-61739-119-4
1. Biography & Autobiography, General
2. Self-Help, Personal Growth, Success
10.08.03

DEDICATION

This book is dedicated to my wonderful wife, Carole. She has been by my side through the worst days as well as the good ones, always giving me the love, encouragement, and support that I needed to stay positive and keep on going. I have had a happy life and consider myself the luckiest of all men because of my incredible good fortune to have her for my wife. I thank God for her.

TABLE OF CONTENTS

INTRODUCTION

Like millions of others in the last couple of decades, I was laid off from a good job that I had held with a large corporation for many years. In my case, it was over twenty-five years with a major oil company in the accounting department of their corporate headquarters. This happened to me back in 1992, and it still amazes me to see how many people have lost their jobs since then and how the trend continues with no end in sight.

At the age of sixty-six, I can look back over numerous life-altering changes that have occurred in our world over my lifetime, and very few have had such a dramatic effect on such a large number of Americans as has this gigantic trend among employers of all kinds towards the reduction in the size of the workforce. Granted, in many cases the employers were driven to cut costs by economic conditions beyond their control. However, I can't resist the urge to mention here the fact that in so many cases, the executives at the top of the ladder continued taking huge paychecks and bonuses while doing all the cost cutting at the expense of the workers who were actually producing the revenues being generated.

Having personally endured the trauma of a layoff and surviving it surprisingly well, I am writing this account of my experiences in the hope that it will encourage others who are going through this to not give up, but keep hope alive and face each new day with the knowledge that there are better days ahead. I promise you that an optimistic outlook along with the determination to keep on going no matter how hard it gets will lead to a life in the future that is far better than the tough times you are facing today.

Here is my story.

BACKGROUND- THE GOOD YEARS

I have never understood why I have been so very lucky my whole life. I never felt like I had done anything to deserve such good fortune as has always been mine. As I tell my story, you'll see how even when bad things happened, I always seemed to come out okay and usually better off than before.

Upon finishing two years of junior college in my home town of Independence, Kansas,

I ignored the advice of everyone around me to complete a four-year degree program at a college in a town not far away. That is what several of my friends and classmates were doing. Instead, I joined an Army Reserve unit, did my stint at Basic Training, then began my civilian career pursuit while fulfilling a six-year Army Reserve program meeting one night a week and two weeks of camp each summer. This went on from 1964 to 1970.

My first full-time job was working in a small, local brokerage office, a branch of a Kansas City firm. I performed various clerical duties while studying for the exams I would take to become a licensed, professional stock broker. I passed all the exams but soon learned that I would never sell enough stock in my small town to make a living at it.

It was during this time that I was blessed with some of that tremendous luck I mentioned at the start. A good buddy of mine had a sister who introduced me to the girl who would later become my wife. We married in 1966, and she has been with me through thick and thin. I still don't know how I could have been so blessed. I think that very few people are fortunate enough to enjoy a marriage as good as ours has been.

When we started our life together, she had a job, but I would soon be leaving the brokerage business without really knowing what I would do. I guess we were too young to know that we should be scared. I looked for a job for a few months. Then one day my father-in-law and I drove about fifty miles to Bartlesville, Oklahoma, the headquarters of Phillips Petroleum Company, and I walked in and applied for a job. I did not have a college degree, but I had all the accounting courses offered in two years, and I was hired on the spot for a position as an accounting clerk in the Exploration and Production Accounting Department.

There was no such thing as "Human Resources" in those days. It was the head of the Personnel Department who interviewed me. He asked me how much money I would need to go to work there. My father ran his own car painting and repair business and he took home $100 a week to support Mom and three kids. I figured that if I could just make $100 a week I would be on top of the world and never have to worry about a thing.

I told the personnel man that I would like to have $400 a month. He asked me if it would be all right if they paid me $450 a month and I just about fell over. He told me to report for work on the following Monday. I was so excited on the drive home that I don't know what kept me from wrecking the car. I called my wife to tell her the good news, and she passed it on to my mother. When told about the starting salary of $450 per month, my mother said, "Oh no dear, he must have misunderstood. They surely won't pay him that much."

As the years passed by, I worked hard and moved from one accounting job to another in the Exploration and Production Department and then the Chemicals Division and back again, getting raises every year and promotions once in a while. I eventually went from the accounting clerk classification and hourly status to the accountant level and a salaried position as an "exempt" employee. I spent seventeen years working in International Accounting. I never got very high on the corporate ladder, but I did go farther than many of those who did have college degrees. During my twenty-five years at Phillips I went from a starting yearly pay of $5,400 to $53,640 at the end. It was a comfortable life that provided us the means to raise our two children in nice neighborhoods and in a middle-class style. We brought a son into the world in 1969 and a daughter in 1972 and they have both made us proud.

I had not been at Phillips very long when that Personnel Manager who hired me invited my wife and me to his home for dinner and Bible study. My wife and I had been raised in different Protestant denominations, and we were adrift spiritually at the time, not attending services anywhere. Had that invitation come from anyone else, I probably would have declined, but I didn't dare say no to the man who had just hired me.

A person's life consists of the physical, the emotional, and the spiritual. It is the spiritual that is often neglected and yet so very important in helping us get through those tough times that life throws our way, not the least of which is losing one's job. Here again is a point in my life where luck or providence or something stepped in to add the greatest blessing of all to my life.

We went to his house for dinner and Bible study about once a week and went to church services with him and his wife at the small congregation where they were members. This went on for a few months. We were very impressed with how warm and welcoming everyone at that church was and felt at home right away. More than that, though, was how shocked we were to learn from our study just how far from the teaching of Scripture our respective denominations had drifted. We suddenly had to face the fact that through the years we had just accepted what we heard at church services and Sunday school without really seeing what the Bible said. We saw that nearly everything we had learned in the past had come from the literature of our respective denominations and not directly from the Bible. The contradictions were shocking, and we were amazed at how little we knew about the Bible after all those years of attendance at church, Sunday school, and youth groups.

It was in June of 1967 that our conversion was complete and we were baptized into Christ. For years we had just gone through the motions of a Christian life, but now it became something real and meaningful and life-changing. As the years passed we would face losing parents and other loved ones and various difficulties that everyone goes through including the job layoff. It was our faith and the support of our church family that gave us the strength to get through it all. We often think about how difficult those days sometimes were. We know that without our faith they would have been much more difficult.

The Protestant denominations all came from the Reformation period starting in the sixteenth century. They were an attempt to reform the Catholic Church. The church we had been lucky enough to find, however, sprang from the Restoration Movement, the effort to restore the New Testament church. It is called the Church of Christ because that name is scriptural (Romans 16:16, Galatians 1:22), and it uses only the Bible for doctrine and practice as it aims to be that original New Testament church. I recommend it to you, knowing how important it has been to me as I have faced life's troubles. Now let's get back to the job.

The highlight of my years at Phillips was the travel I got to experience. It started with a few trips from Bartlesville to Houston. Then later I was sent to Cali, Colombia, South America and then to Mexico City, and Lagos, Nigeria. Most of these trips were not all that important from a business need. Back in those days, big companies were very liberal with their travel budgets sending employees all over the world to handle problems that could often have been handled by phone or fax.

The very first business trip was an interesting experience. It was the first time I got to fly in a big jet airplane and my first visit to Houston, a very big place for a small town boy like me. At the Houston airport, I rented a car and got directions to the office building I would be visiting. It was around midnight and the hotel where I would be staying was right next door to the office building. After a forty-five minute trip by car in the dark, I found the hotel and office building and pulled in, feeling very relieved. However, at the hotel desk, I was told that they had sold my room even though it had been on a guaranteed reservation and they had nothing else available. They called other hotels, but there was a big convention in town, and they could find nothing available anywhere in the city. Then I told them I was going to sleep on a couch in the hotel lobby, so they came up with a deal. They had a room that was permanently rented by another oil company and used only for daytime meetings. No one ever slept there, so they said I could use that room if I didn't mess up their brochures and they would move me to another room the next day. We had a deal, and this was the beginning of my travel adventures on behalf of the company.

The trip to Cali, Colombia was little more than a tour of a carbon black producing plant and getting acquainted with the local office staff. Carbon Black is the primary ingredient in the manufacture of tires. Cali sits near the west coast of the country of Colombia in South America and is a very beautiful place. There were the rich people who had servants and the poor people who served them and almost no one in between. One memorable day was spent having lunch at a Country Club where our manager was a member, followed by the viewing of horses being taken through a series of jumps in some kind of equestrian competition. It was all in a beautiful setting, and it was fun to live like the rich, if only for a day.

My main mission in Mexico City was to gather information about the tax consequences of the way we structured the salary of the manager of the local office. When I reported my findings to my manager back home, he was skeptical of them and called the Mexican office manager to check it out. When he was told exactly what I had told him, he just grunted and dismissed me from his office. This was while I worked in the Chemicals Division. A short time later I was asked by the manager of the International Accounting staff in the Natural Resources Group (another name for Exploration & Production) if I would be interested in a job over there, and I jumped at the chance, feeling under-appreciated where I was. It was September 1, 1978 when I made this move.

The most interesting trip came in 1987, when I went to Nigeria where we were closing a branch office and negotiating severance packages with all the employees. We also had to dispose of a large fleet of automobiles, including the gold Mercedes Benz that had been used by the

Branch Manager there in Lagos. I was there for three weeks, the longest of all my trips. On the flight home, I extended the layover in London to include a night in a London hotel and one day of fast and furious sightseeing. A business associate and friend from our London office took me around town that day. We managed to see Westminster Abbey, St. Paul's Cathedral (where Prince Charles and Lady Diana were married), the Tower of London (where they keep the crown jewels), and the front of Buckingham Palace. They did not give tours inside the Palace in those days as I think they do now. The day ended with a boat ride from the Tower of London down the River Thames to Big Ben which was near my hotel. It was a very exhausting but exciting day.

I am grateful for the experiences I had in international travel. It is a great thing to get a taste of other cultures and peoples whose lives are entirely different from ours. Especially in visiting very poor countries and touring their filthy market places, you can gain a new appreciation for the good life we have always taken for granted in America. The people we call poor in this country would be called rich in many parts of the world. To have one indoor bathroom with running water is a luxury many of the world's poorest can only dream of. Maybe seeing how little the people in some places have made it easier to deal with the problems I had after losing my job. I came back to a comfortable life after some of those trips feeling very rich as I drove my nice car from my nice home to my office each day, where I worked in air-conditioned comfort at my desk and computer.

My wife, Carole, and I were married in March of 1966, and we moved to Bartlesville in October. We rented a small apartment right downtown about two blocks from the building I started working in at Phillips. We lived there for about two years and then, in 1968, we bought our first house, a modest two bedroom, one bath, frame house with a carport at the whopping price of $10,000. In August of 1969 our son was born, and we were in that house for about two and one-half years. Then, in about 1971, we bought our second house. It was a three bedroom brick house with one bathroom and a one car garage, and its price was $15,000. I think it had about 1,500 square feet of living space.

One year at Thanksgiving time, there was a co-worker from China in town on business and we invited him to have dinner with us on that holiday. He looked around our house and said "Is all of this just for the four of you?" We lived there for six or seven years, and our daughter was born during that time, in June of 1972. Then in 1977, we really moved up. We bought a brand new brick house in a great neighborhood out on the east side at a cost of about $56,000 and sold the previous house for around $21,000. This was a really nice house with four bedrooms, two and one-half bathrooms, a formal dining room, a den with a fireplace, and an unusually large living room. The living space was about 2,100 square feet, and we thought we had really made it. The job was going well, I was getting raises pretty often, and life was good. We stayed in that house for thirteen years, then moved one more time in 1990 to a three bedroom, two bath, house in another nice neighborhood still out on the east side of town. Through these years we had built up home equity of about $25,000. I didn't realize how fast it could all come tumbling down when the layoffs came.

The solid foundation for the life that I was so blessed to have consisted of two parts: First in importance, though not in order of time, was the faith in God I had found through the Bible study I had always neglected in the past. The second part of it was the great marriage I had to a wife who would be right there with me in the tough times as well as the good ones. She never let me feel that being laid off was due to any failure on my part, and always gave me encouragement and support. We have been together through all of life's challenges, and I can't imagine what my life would have been like without her at my side.

From our marriage in 1966 up to the end of the Phillips years in 1992, life was good. We had two great children and our church home, where we stayed busy with various activities, as well as little league and PTA and all those things with our children. Then came the layoffs. Our lives would be drastically changed.

DOOMSDAY—
THE LAYOFF

In the spring of 1992, Phillips was laying off lots of people in the offices in Bartlesville. There had been other layoffs going back a few years, but they had mostly affected people working in plants and branch offices in other states and countries. My greatest fault was in being so naïve. I had always had good performance reviews and been a good employee, so I thought it wouldn't happen to me. It was sad to see some of those people I knew lose their jobs, but I just could not believe it would actually happen to me. Even on the day when it had been announced that they would be going through my department laying off some of those in my immediate area, I still thought I would keep my job.

When my manager tapped me on the shoulder and asked me to go with her to her office, there was no doubt about what was happening. I guess I was kind of numb, as it seemed like it was in a dream and not reality. I was seated in the office with someone from Human Resources who explained some of what was happening and told me to go to my desk and get only the few things I might need immediately. I was then to report to another floor where I would join others to receive further information before leaving the building. I would have to make an appointment with my supervisor to come back and clean out my desk on another day. All of this was just a little bit humiliating.

As I returned to my desk to get a few things, those around me were looking very sad. There were even a few tears and a hug or two. Then I went to the assigned place for the explanation of outplacement services, severance packages, and things offered by the company to assist us in our departure from the company. I knew that finding other employment would be very difficult for me because I lacked a degree and had experience limited only to the oil business. As the time for layoffs approached my department, there had been much talk about what people would do if they were among those laid off. Some of my co-workers had a pretty good idea of what things they might pursue. I was not so lucky. I had absolutely no idea whatsoever of what I could do if I lost my job. I have never in my life felt so totally lost and helpless as I did then.

The company established outplacement centers on two sides of town. Those who were laid off, about 1,100 of us altogether, could go there and get the use of free long-distance phone lines, newspapers from most major cities, and even counselors who could help with polishing a resume. I went there daily for some time, but made no progress and soon felt defeated. I sent out a lot of resumes, but I did not get any interviews. I was forty-eight years old and not very marketable. With twenty-five years at Phillips

I had been accustomed to five weeks vacation a year, excellent life and health insurance plans, retirement benefits, and a stock savings plan. Now, I had nothing.

Looking around at the others coming to the center each day, I saw that they were nearly all around my age or older. It was clear that older workers were being targeted because they could be replaced with younger people who could be paid much less in salary and benefits. Those days of looking at newspaper ads and sending out resumes were dark, depressing days. I am thankful that I had my wife and my church to offer support, comfort, and encouragement when I really needed it. Without them, I don't know what I would have done.

There was one bright spot that I had going for me that not everyone who loses their job has, and that was a generous severance package. Due to the unusually large number of people being laid off, Phillips was offering an enhanced severance package in addition to the regular severance package that would always be available. It was based on years of service, and because I had been there for twenty-five years, I received a very sizable lump-sum payment. It totaled nearly $80,000, before taxes, and we would need it to get through the next two years without having a good job.

Not everyone who loses their job in these tough times will be as lucky as I was to get a sizeable severance package. This enabled us to pay the bills and survive in relative comfort until a steady paycheck came along. Others may have to live with relatives or take other steps to survive if another job isn't found pretty quickly. Although most people would apply for unemployment benefits to get by on until finding a new job, I never did that because I had the severance pay. I also had some confidence that I would be working at something soon, even if it was far less than the job I lost. I still had to face the fact that this cushion would eventually run out and I desperately needed to find another job. Bartlesville was pretty much a one-company town, and it was clear that my next career would not begin there.

Another bright spot in our situation was the fact that our two children were out of the nest by the time the layoff came for me. Our son, Randy, had graduated from Spartan School of Aeronautics and was living on his own and getting started in his own small business. Our daughter, Lori, was a Freshman at Oklahoma State University in Stillwater, Oklahoma. If we still had children at home when the layoff came, things would have been even harder, particularly with all the moves we would be making as the hunt for employment continued. Little did we know then how many twists and turns our search would take.

FLOUNDERING AROUND IN THE DARK

My wife and I had spent most of our lives in southeast Kansas and northeast Oklahoma. We had both seen all of the ice and snow we ever wanted to see, and I had no desire to scrape ice off the windshield ever again. Having vacationed in Florida several times over those last twenty-five years and loving it more than anywhere else we had ever been, deciding where to go was a no-brainer. We thought we could be unemployed and poor in beautiful Florida just as well as anyplace else. The layoff came in March of 1992, and we moved to Tampa in May. Our daughter was in college at Oklahoma State University in Stillwater, and she lived there during the school year and could come to be with us in the summer. We even planned for her to transfer to a college in Tampa for the next term. During her visit that summer of 1992, we filled out the papers for her application to school there in the fall. Those plans came crashing down when she told us that she was dating a fellow who might be "Mister Right," so she wanted to stay in Oklahoma long enough to find out. Sure enough, he was the one, so she never moved to Florida. She graduated in May of 1995 and they were married in October of 1996. We had also assumed that after our daughter moved to Florida, our son would come also. That too failed to work out, so the downside of living there was being so far from our kids. We know that many people live far from their grown kids for various reasons, but for us it was always difficult and we always longed to be closer to them.

We made a preliminary trip to Tampa to find a house before making the final move with all of our furniture and belongings. We found a nice three bedroom, two bath, house in Tampa that we could rent for about $750 per month. We also had a mortgage payment on the house in Bartlesville, and a real need to get it sold. We moved into our rented house in Tampa and began our quest for some way to make a living, not knowing that it would be a two-year ordeal.

We had seen a newspaper ad for an opportunity to get into the vending business that sounded really good, and the chance to run our own business out of our home was really appealing. We had money from the severance package to buy the vending boxes and candy and get started, so we went for it. It was not a smart move. These candy boxes were tied to a charity and the money for the candy was deposited on the honor system. You guessed it, most people would take a fistful of candy and deposit little or no money. Did I say earlier that I was a little naïve? We drove our own car all over Tampa and St. Petersburg tending to about two hundred of those boxes for several months, making very little money until we saw that we had to get out of it. Did I say earlier that I have been lucky all my life? Believe it or not, we actually got the people who sold us those boxes in the first place to take them back and give us a full refund. I could not believe our good fortune, but we were still unemployed and making no money.

You will remember that I said 1,100 people were laid off in Bartlesville in 1992. Guess what happened to the real estate market in that town? It really went south. I don't know how many times I called our real estate agent to see if there were any offers on our house.

Each time the answer was "no" and we had to drop the asking price again. With a rent payment in Tampa and a mortgage payment in Bartlesville each month and no real money coming in, it was plain to see that we had to do whatever it took to get rid of the house in Bartlesville. We finally had to drop the price so much that we took a loss on it and had to send a check to the closing. After twenty-five years of living the "American Dream," owning a home, and building up about $25,000 in equity, we lost every bit of it and found ourselves no better off financially than if we had rented all those years.

Now, on the bright side, and there always is one if you look for it, we had those twenty-five good years. Our kids had the nice house to live in with the fenced backyard, the puppy dogs when they were growing up, and a place to invite their friends for social get-togethers. We had a nice home for holiday dinners with family and friends and a place where the youth group from church could come for devotionals and games. The houses we lived in provided no return from an investment perspective, but they served as a backdrop for a happy life. Many times I have heard it said that a house is a person's best investment. If that's your best investment, you are in big trouble and you will have to work till you drop. However, a house is a good place to raise a family, and we were fortunate to have one during those years when we needed it most.

The other bright spot during our time in Tampa was the church home we found. It was a small congregation of maybe around eighty people. They were extremely warm and friendly to us and made us feel immediately at home. The elders and preacher were very serious about teaching sound doctrine that was faithful to the scriptures, just as was the case back in Bartlesville, Oklahoma, and we loved our new church home.

Well, the vending business was over, the house in Bartlesville had finally sold, and now it was time to do something else–but what?

WHEN DESPERATE, TRY ANYTHING

My wife was able to get a job with an electronics supply company in Tampa, so that helped, but it was far short of what we needed to make ends meet. I needed a job and was not able to land a good one any time soon. We both thought we would like to get in the business of real estate appraisal. We did not want to be in sales but thought the appraisal work would be good. We both took the required course to get registered and did well with the class work. She was not able to find employment in the field, and it was clear that being a female was a major deterrent for her. I did find a job with a local real estate firm, and found the work to be interesting and enjoyable. I liked the work, which involved measuring a house, drawing its floor plan to scale, taking pictures of comparable houses in the neighborhood that had sold recently, and writing a detailed report of the differences between the target house and the comparable sales to arrive at an appraised value for the target house. There were, however, some problems that proved insurmountable.

The state laws were very stringent. They required a registered appraiser to put in a two-year apprenticeship with a certified appraiser before he could get certified and work independently. I was doing that but I soon found that I could never make a decent income at it. A typical appraisal fee was about $275. The head of the real estate firm got the first slice of that, then the certified appraiser I was working with got the next biggest piece, and I wound up with the little bit that was left over. With the research time, travel, measuring, and report writing, it was not possible to do more than one job a day and do it right. It became apparent that I could not make enough money to continue as an apprentice long enough to get certified. It was time to try something else.

The next few jobs I tried were sales jobs. I had always been skeptical of those because there was no guarantee of income, just commissions based on sales. Because I was not finding any real jobs available for which I felt qualified, I decided to try some sales jobs out of sheer desperation. Remember what I said in the introduction about never giving up, but being determined to keep on trying no matter how hard it gets? That is where I was at this time.

I tried selling jewelry, not in a nice store, but out on the street, going from one business to another, trying to sell jewelry to employees from a pouch I carried around. Now *that* was desperate and it didn't last very long.

Next, I walked into a new car dealership and asked for a job selling cars. The manager said he would give me a try, but that lasted only a few days. I sat around the showroom for several days waiting for some training and guidance that did not seem to be coming so I just told him to forget it and walked out.

Another desperate attempt we both made was answering an ad from a telemarketing company to work nights. Our job was to call people who had filled out cards at state fairs to tell them they had won a cruise to the Bahamas. All they had to do was "get themselves down to Ft. Lauderdale" from wherever in the country they lived to get a short cruise over to the Bahamas for a couple of days of fun and a timeshare sales pitch. Very few people decided that it was a good deal, so we only lasted a couple of weeks before bailing out of that job.

After that I saw an ad for a company needing people to sell water softener equipment. That was a riot. They had ladies making calls during the day to set appointments in the evening for us salesmen to demonstrate the equipment in peoples' homes. The sales talk and product demonstration took about ninety minutes or more and was really quite convincing. We filled a test tube with water from their faucet and another with water from the same faucet that we put through our filter. Then we put chemical drops in each test tube that would make any minerals in the water settle to the bottom of the tube. The prospects could see all the gunk in the bottom of the test tube that had water straight from their faucets compared to the crystal clear water in the tube with the water that had passed through our filter. The problem was that our equipment was very expensive. It was a big whole-house system that cost about $4,000, or a total more like $7,000 if they financed it.

My sales commission was very good, and I could make some real money if successful. Surprisingly, I did very well the first month. I sold several systems and made a lot of money. If I could do that every month, I would be doing great. I never quite understood what happened next. After one very successful month, it seemed I could not sell another one to save my life. For several months, I went out every night from one appointment to another doing demonstrations when I could get in the door but almost never closed a sale. I think the early success made me stick with it longer than I should have. I kept thinking I would be successful again, but it just didn't happen. Several months went by with almost no income before I finally gave it up. I finally figured that I was showing the people that they needed something for their water, but they went out and found something a lot cheaper. The system was a good one, and we had one at our house, but it was a more expensive system than most people could afford. It was definitely time to move on to something else.

Now I should say that during this dreadful two-year period from the layoff in March of 1992 to February of 1994, we did have some fun even though secure employment had eluded us. We spent the fourth of July in 1992 at Harbor Island in Tampa. This was a happening place back in those days, and the harbor was full of beautiful boats and lots of people who were there to enjoy the day and watch the fireworks that night. Later in the month of July we spent a few days at Anna Maria Island just off of Bradenton, Florida and also at Clearwater Beach, a place that would become an all-time favorite we would visit again many times over the next several years.

Other good times came when our children and other family members were able to come for a visit with us. We loved those visits and the things we were able to show our loved ones, but we still never saw them as often as we would have liked.

Our son, Randy, and daughter, Lori, came to Tampa to be with us at Christmas of 1992. Lori was back again in June of 1993, and we celebrated her twenty-first birthday at a restaurant on the causeway called Castaways. When Christmas of 1993 rolled around, we went back to Bartlesville, Oklahoma to be with our kids and other family members in the area. We had Christmas dinner at the home of Carole's brother, Bill, and his wife, Elaine, in Independence, Kansas. Joining us there were Randy and Lori and Bill's and Elaine's daughter, Elese, with her husband, John, and daughter, Brooke, and also my Mom and Dad.

Even though we thoroughly enjoyed living in Florida with the beaches and the seafood and all the great places to explore, there were always two big clouds over everything. First, we missed our kids and other family members, and second, we could not forget for a minute that we had not yet landed the steady, secure employment that we so desperately needed. By February of 1994, the severance money was nearly gone and I was still jobless, but thanks to God that was about to change.

FINALLY LANDING A REAL JOB

Finally something came along that promised a steady income, a roof over our heads, and three meals a day. There was an ad in the paper for a couple to work together helping manage a retirement center. This company was unique in the retirement industry in the way they operated. They hired one couple as managers and another couple as co-managers to operate retirement centers that offered independent living for seniors who did not need a nursing home environment. They provided each couple with a very nice apartment to live in rent free, three meals a day with the residents in the dining room, free housekeeping, and a pretty nice salary with health insurance and a 401-K plan as well. Each couple worked alone on the other couple's days off and both couples worked together a few days each week. It was a pretty nice arrangement in that the two couples could trade off covering for each other when one of them needed to change days off or add a day or two on occasion.

This particular job was for a co-manager team at a beautiful facility in Clearwater, Florida, about ten minutes from the beach. We drove over there and looked at the place and talked to the managers about the job. Later, we went to interview with the regional manager, whose office was in Ormond Beach on the east coast. He offered us the job and told us that he was going to put us in as co-managers at Clearwater. He would then fire the managers and replace them with some experienced co-managers from a facility in Naples, Florida. This was in February of 1994, and it was the first time since the layoff in March of 1992 that we had a steady income to count on and the feeling of security. By this time our severance package money was all gone and we were at the end of our rope. We had a huge garage sale, downsizing from our three bedroom house, and moved into our lovely two bedroom apartment at the Clearwater retirement center.

After two years of bouncing from one failed career attempt after another while running through the nest-egg, it was a tremendous relief to finally have a job that seemed to promise the security we so desperately needed.

This job was different from anything we had ever before envisioned, and there were some very positive aspects to it. First of all, we had a place to live rent-free where we could work together as a team each day with steady paychecks and health insurance and all the usual benefits, as well as free food to boot. We also no longer needed two cars, so that eliminated one car and one car insurance bill. Now I realize that probably not all couples would work together every day and get along very well, but remember I was the lucky guy with the great marriage, and for Carole and me, it was perfect. We enjoyed working together and applied ourselves diligently to the job. Sometimes we would take a bus-load of residents out on a picnic at one of the area's gorgeous parks, leaving the other couple to hold down the fort, and we had a great time.

On our days off we went sightseeing all over the state of Florida. Occasionally, some of our family would come down to visit, and we would enjoy showing them some of the sights. In March of 1994 our son and daughter came for a visit, and we showed them all around the Tampa Bay area.

A highlight of that visit was the canoe trip the four of us took down the Hillsborough River starting at Lettuce Lake Park in Tampa. What made this canoe experience so special were the alligators in the river with us at the first part of the trip. They swam beside the canoe and dove under it, but did not give us any trouble. In addition, there were the beautiful, big herons and egrets and other birds we saw along the way and the tropical foliage and natural beauty all around us. This is what they call "the real Florida," the part away from the theme parks and commercial tourist attractions.

A luncheon cruise down the intra-coastal waterway at Clearwater was also a must-do when visitors came. My parents came to see us in April, and we took them to the Ringling Brothers Museum and Home in Sarasota on my mother's seventy-seventh birthday, which was April 5. In May we had a visit by Carole's brother, John, and her niece, Elese, with her husband, John, and daughter, Brooke, that included a trip to Disney World in Orlando. In June, Carole and I drove down to Key West and fell in love with that area. Then in July 1994, our son and daughter came back for another visit and our sightseeing with them included the Ringling estate at Sarasota.

We loved the beach, the seafood, and the wildlife, including egrets and pelicans and alligators; we just took it all in every chance we got. Some mornings, on our days off, we would go over to the beach and have breakfast at a hotel restaurant that overlooked the beach. Then we would take a leisurely stroll right by the water. At this time of day it was not usually crowded. This was the most relaxing and stress reducing thing we had ever done. I loved thinking about the tourists who were there to enjoy this for just a week or two before returning to their homes in the north, and it made me feel so good just realizing that we got to live there all the time.

Do you remember what I said in the introduction about being optimistic and determined to keep on trying even when times are tough and that there would be better days ahead? Now, for the first time since the layoff two years in the past, I felt like we did have a better life and Phillips did me a favor when they kicked me out.

The work as co-managers was different from anything either of us had ever done before. It was almost like running our own business in some ways. We had payrolls to handle and a budget to control and employees to supervise. We dealt with maintenance men and landscape people and various vendors. The other managers treated us like equals and especially when they were off, we were running this big business without anyone overseeing us. Regional managers and other bigshots from the company came in once in a while, but not very often.

We interacted a lot with the residents. During meals there were servers to handle the food, but we would go around to all the tables pouring coffee and visiting with everyone.

I would drive the bus and take residents to doctor appointments. My wife would lead them in various activities such as Bingo. We got very attached to some of them, but believe it or not, some of those old folks could get pretty grouchy. Then we had to put on a smile and our "diplomatic hats" and try to settle them down. It was challenging, but fun.

As you might guess, the job had its negative side too. We had to hire, fire, and supervise cooks, dishwashers, housekeepers, and various other employees. Sometimes in the middle of the night the alarm would sound in our apartment. That usually meant that one of our elderly residents had fallen, and I would have to go to their apartment and pick them up and make sure they were all right. Sometimes a resident would die, and we would attend the funeral and often take a bus-load of residents along with us. Sometimes they would want the funeral to be held right in our facility, so we would help organize that. Even with these negative aspects of our new career, the positives mentioned earlier seemed to make it all worthwhile.

Enjoyable as it was most of the time, there was this one big drawback and that was being so far from our kids and other family members back in Oklahoma and Kansas. We had been separated by 1,400 miles for more than two years and just could not get together nearly often enough. Our son and daughter were in Oklahoma, and my parents were living in Independence, Kansas. Carole's brother, Bill; his wife, Elaine; their daughter, Elese; her husband, John; and their daughter, Brooke, were all living in or near Independence. In addition, my older brother, Gary, was living in Oklahoma City at that time.

In August of 1994 after being at the Clearwater retirement center for only six months, we seized the opportunity to transfer to one of the company's nice properties in Austin, Texas. That put us a lot closer to all of our family, and we enjoyed living in Austin. It gave us a lot of new places to discover in some of the prettiest hill country in Texas. When family members came to visit us, we had a whole new bunch of places to show them, including the capitol building, the LBJ Presidential Library at the University of Texas, and the Johnson Ranch.

Our son and daughter came to be with us for Christmas of 1994. In April of 1995 we entertained Carole's brother, Bill, and his family, Elaine, Elese, John, and Brooke. That same month, we had a visit by my parents. My mother would be out of breath after walking just a short distance, and did not seem to be in very good health. Little did we know that in just two months she would die.

During the period of about May through September each year, Austin has another outstanding attraction, and that is bats. Yes, bats, millions of them. They nest under the Congress Avenue Bridge, right at the edge of downtown, and come out to feed every evening at about sundown. Crowds gather on the bridge, on both banks of the river and in boats on the river, to watch the amazing sight of all these bats flying out from under the bridge to begin their daily hunt for food. They come out in swarms that continue for at least thirty minutes or more. They eat tons of insects, and that's a good thing.

Another of Austin's hot spots is the Oasis Restaurant. It is an amazing facility which sits at the top of a hill overlooking Lake Travis, and it has about thirty decks along the hillside for outside dining, as well as lots of space for inside dining too. The view is terrific, and we have dined there with family members on many occasions. The buildings and grounds are beautifully decorated with lots of outstanding sculptures that make the whole place a feast for the eyes.

We also got along well with the manager couple, found another church home, and settled into a good life once again. As in Florida, this job was a mixture of good and bad, as I guess all of life really is.

Hiring and keeping good employees was one of the most difficult things. Many times the dishwasher would not show up for work, and I spent the day doing the dishwasher's job. Once we decided that a dishwasher needed to be fired. I went back to the kitchen and found that I had to wake him up to fire him. Another time, the head cook and I had a disagreement over when the activities director could have her lunch, and he decided to challenge my authority. He said he would quit so I said that would be fine, and he walked out right in the middle of the lunch meal.

We had to scramble to hire a replacement, but it was worth it.

Perhaps the most memorable occasion was the morning one of our lady residents was found dead on the floor next to her bed. This facility was mostly independent living, but it did have an assisted-living wing too, so there was a nurse available to assist with this situation. Once a policeman and two guys from the funeral home were ready to remove her, I had to avert a disaster. Her apartment was on the second floor and they were going to wheel her out on a gurney down the hall to the elevator right past a group of residents who were being entertained by a musician in a common area. I said, "Oh no, we can't do that!" So I got on one corner of the gurney and the policeman and two guys from the funeral home got the other three corners and we carried the gurney with the body on it down an outside staircase.

In spite of a few bad situations like those just described, we mostly enjoyed our lives in Austin. We worked well with the manager couple, enjoyed the residents, and treated the new life in Austin as an exciting new adventure. Here again, we thought we could say that losing the job at Phillips had been a good thing that led us to a better new life in spite of the pitfalls along the way. We continued as co-managers in Austin from August of 1994 to May of 1995, and then we made a bad decision. The manager couple at one of the properties in Arlington, Texas was retiring and we had the opportunity to take that job. It would be a promotion to manager level and would also put us even closer to the family in Oklahoma and Kansas. So we went for it.

DISAPPOINTMENT SETS IN

This move started out badly and did not get any better. On June 1, 1995, we pulled into the Arlington property in our U-Haul truck loaded with everything we owned and were immediately told that we needed to call my sister, Linda, who lived in the Denver area. She said that my mother had a stroke and was in the hospital in Independence, Kansas. We unloaded the truck into our apartment as fast as we could, turned in the truck, and drove our car to Independence. We stayed a couple of days while mother lingered in the hospital, and then returned to Arlington to unpack our belongings and start our new job as managers. After a few more days, word came that mother was probably near death, so we went back to Independence to be with her and the rest of our family. She died on June 10, at the age of seventy-eight. After the funeral a few days later, we returned to Arlington to begin our new job again.

As co-managers in Austin, we had less pressure and stress from those higher up in the company, but as managers in Arlington we got all the heat. Pressure to keep all apartments rented and all operations, such as the kitchen and house-keeping services, ticking like clockwork was intense. Meeting company standards was not just difficult, it was impossible. For example, staffing for housekeeping allowed only fifteen to twenty minutes for cleaning each apartment, bathroom, and all. Not surprisingly, residents were not happy with the results. The time allowed for preparing and serving meals and getting the dining room and kitchen perfectly cleaned afterwards was equally ridiculous. It finally hit us that

that if a company has a huge employee turnover rate, there could be a reason for it. After just six months, we could see that another change was necessary due to the extreme pressure and stress. We liked Austin a lot better than Arlington, and the company had more properties there with many more jobs available.

So in November of 1995, we asked for, and received, a transfer back to Austin as co-managers of one of the retirement centers there and immediately began our search for a different line of work. One of the positives of this type of work was the fact that it included a company provided apartment. That could also be a negative, however, because leaving the job also meant losing your only home. Therefore, we definitely could not afford to leave this company until other employment was found.

TRY, TRY AGAIN

The co-managers we had at Arlington had gotten interested in the mini-storage business and suggested we try that. It was similar in some ways to what we had been doing because a couple could work together and live on-site in a company-provided apartment. The big company in Austin was Public Storage with thirteen properties just in Austin.

In December of 1995, after only a month back in Austin, we went to work for Public Storage at one of their facilities on Austin's south side. It was an older property located next to a salvage yard that smashed old cars, but we didn't care about that. The big thing was the huge reduction in the stress we felt. It was so great to just be on our own with no employees to worry about hiring, firing, and supervising. A relief manager would come in two days a week so we could have our days off, and we felt like this was a far better life than what we had come from. Once again, we thought that in spite of the difficulties along the way, we had reached a point where we could be thankful for the layoff at Phillips.

We dug into the training for our new career in the storage business and settled into our new apartment, which was connected to our new office. When Christmas of 1995 came around, we celebrated with Carole's brother, Bill, and his wife, Elaine, at their house in Independence, Kansas. Joining us there were our kids, Randy and Lori, my Dad and brother, Gary, and John, Elese, and Brooke. We were in this new job only a few months when we had the opportunity to transfer to another Public Storage property in a better neighborhood on Austin's north side, so we did that.

We soon learned that many couples who had been with our old retirement company had gone from there to the storage business in recent years. One such couple worked down the street from us with a company called Private Mini Storage. They kept telling us how much better their company was than ours and encouraging us to switch. It wasn't very long before we got a call from the owner of that company wanting us to consider working for them in Mobile, Alabama. One of his regional managers came to Austin to interview us, and the offer we got was too good to refuse.

NEW JOB, START OVER AGAIN

In August of 1996, after only eight months with Public Storage, we moved to Mobile. This would take us farther away from our family, but it offered more money and a location near the beach in the South that we loved so much. One good thing about living in these places far from family was that it gave them a place to vacation and be hosted by us in areas they might otherwise never get to see.

In case you are starting to think that after being in Bartlesville for twenty-five years we were sure doing a lot of moving around, you would be right. Old friends from Bartlesville began to wonder about it. On a Christmas card one year, a lady noted that it looked like we were "on the lam." We started to joke that we were in the Federal Witness Protection Program. As difficult as all this moving was, we did look at it as a new adventure and opportunity to see and do things that would otherwise not be possible for us. Even though life in Bartlesville had been so much more stable and secure (I thought), we were now experiencing a much richer, fuller life and appreciating the positive aspects of it. Don't forget what I said in the introduction about the importance of having an optimistic outlook and the determination to keep on going. I have discovered through all of this how important attitude is in determining how happy a life you will have, and faith in God is a big part of that.

When I started working for Phillips Petroleum Company in 1966, it wasn't long until my first supervisor and a friend of his retired. They started work there on the same day and retired together on the same day forty years later. I thought I would be at Phillips that long too. The layoff really turned my life upside down. Looking back now, I can see what a blessing the layoff really was. There were difficult times and sleepless nights worrying about how we would make a living. Sometimes I was working very hard and getting nowhere, but I never gave up. When one thing failed to work out, I tried something else. What I learned along the way was that this new life of ours included a lot of good times and blessings along with the negative aspects. In fact, when I look back at all that happened, I can honestly say that the good things far outweighed the bad.

We got to see a lot of neat things and meet a lot of great people as we moved around from place to place. Living in different parts of the country is something I would recommend to anyone. In fact, I can't think of anything more boring than spending your whole life in one place. I know that some people are fine with that and find comfort and security in it, but it is just not for me. I guess I have more of an adventurous side than would be easily seen in me. The opportunity to be a part of some wonderful church congregations in different areas was one of the best things we experienced. Every place we went, Christians welcomed us to be part of their church family and helped us to grow our faith.

Not long after our move to Mobile our daughter, Lori, married that fellow named Stuart, for whom she had stayed in Oklahoma. That was on October 26, 1996 in Stillwater, Oklahoma. Of course, I gave the bride away and our son, Randy, served as an usher. We looked pretty spiffy in our tuxedos. All of the family was there including my sister, Linda, and her husband, Don, from Denver and Carole's brother, John, and his wife, Joyce, from Ruidoso, New Mexico. The relatives from Independence were all there including my Dad and my brother, Gary. Stuart's parents were residents of Stillwater and were instrumental in putting it all together. Many friends and family from his side were there as well.

As with most of the others, there were some very positive things about this job. We loved Mobile and the surrounding area on both sides of Mobile Bay from Pascagoula to Pensacola. There were the beaches, the seafood, the wildlife, and yes, it included alligators. We loved the warm climate, especially in the winter time, the palm trees, and wide variety of tropical plants and flowers. We had a small patio with our apartment and planted a palm tree about one foot tall. The last time we passed by there, that tree was about twelve to fifteen feet tall. There were many great places to visit with a one-day outing such as Antebellum homes, civil war forts, beaches, and Bellingrath Gardens, one of the most outstanding in the country. Our storage property was in a great location near lots of shops, restaurants, and movie theaters. There was a Wal-Mart in walking distance.

We found a great church home at a small place called Spanish Fort just across the seven-mile bridge on the east side of Mobile Bay. Every Sunday we decompressed from the work week by driving across that bridge to Bible class and worship service. I enjoyed teaching an adult Bible class there for about three years. After the worship service ended, we headed to the beach. We would find a place to change into comfortable clothes, choose from among the many wonderful restaurants in the area and spend the afternoon at the beach or cruising around in that area looking for new places to explore and revisiting favorite places we had already discovered.

The main drawback to living so far from family was missing them, so whenever any of them could come for a visit, we really enjoyed it. At Christmas of 1996, our son came to Mobile for a visit. In February of 1997, we had a visit from John, Elese, and Brooke. Then in March of that year our daughter and new son-in-law came down, followed in July by my Dad, who was celebrating his eighty-third birthday. We also had a visit from my wife's brother, Bill, and his wife, Elaine, in July so we got to see a lot of family in just a few months time. We enjoyed taking visitors to see all the sights. Most of them had not ever seen much of this area.

Highlights of these visits always included the battleship USS Alabama, Bellingrath Gardens and Home, and the Naval Air Station at Pensacola. We also usually included a boat ride from Perdito Key down the waterway to the ruins of old Fort McRee where the Gulf of Mexico meets Pensacola Bay. It was a very scenic ride in a small boat, and we always saw dolphins on this trip. That always delighted our guests. Any visitors who came at the right time of year could also enjoy the Mardi Gras festivities with us. They were usually unaware of the fact that the popular U.S version of the old French holiday "Mardi Gras" got its start in Mobile, not New Orleans. We also liked the way the Mobile version was more family oriented than the one in New Orleans.

In August of 1997, Carole and I took a short trip to New Orleans to see the sights there. We especially enjoyed the Aquarium and Zoo. Later that month we were back in Kansas and Oklahoma to see all the kinfolk there. Our son came back for another visit at Christmas time in 1997, and our daughter came in June of 1998 to go on job interviews in preparation for a move to Mobile. Best of all, Lori and Stuart moved to Mobile that year. They had fallen in love with the area just as we had, and it really helped us a lot to have at least part of our family living so close. We spent time with them as often as possible and hoped that Randy and other family members would eventually move down there also.

In April of 1998, Carole and I went out to Ruidoso, New Mexico, to see her brother, John, and his wife, Joyce. Her other brother, Bill, and his wife, Elaine, and our son, Randy, also met us there so we had quite a lot of family together at once and had a great vacation.

Randy came to see us in November of 1998, bringing with him a young lady named Angla (pronounced Angela, but spelled without the e), and her three year old son, Shelby. We took them to the beach at Gulf Shores, Alabama, and it was the first time that Angla and Shelby had seen the ocean. Randy and Angla were planning to marry, and Carole took great joy in helping Angla shop for a wedding dress. They got married in February of 1999. Randy became an instant dad, and we became instant grandparents. The wedding took place in Cushing, Oklahoma, where Angla's parents lived, and all the family was there. Their jobs were in Stillwater, but they soon bought a five-acre property at the edge of Cushing where they have lived since. He is a great dad, and he later adopted Shelby. At Christmas time in 1999, Randy, Angla, and Shelby came back to Mobile for another visit.

August of 1999 found us planning a trip to Denver to see my sister, Linda, and her husband,

Don. We wanted to take a train trip, but there was just one catch. The train from Mobile to Denver took a route through Chicago. It seemed a terrible way to get from point A to point B, but we did it anyway. There was a pretty long layover in Chicago, so we got to do just a little sightseeing there. It was all on foot, but we made it to the top of the Sears tower and down to the park at the shore of Lake Michigan. My sister and brother-in-law always showed us a great time with all the mountain trips and other sights we could fit in to our time schedule, as well as more good food than anyone could possibly eat.

There was one little foul-up at the trip's end. We were to arrive back in Mobile by train very early one morning. Our daughter, Lori, said she would pick us up, but we told her not to do it because it would be at such an awful hour and we could get a taxi. The train had a stop in New Orleans that turned out to be an unusually long delay. We were offered the option of taking a bus the rest of the way in to Mobile which would get us there sooner and leave less time to kill in New Orleans, so we did that. On arrival in Mobile by bus, we got a taxi and went home. We did not know that Lori had called the train station to get the approximate arrival time and then went down there to pick us up arriving just as the train had offloaded its passengers and headed on to Pensacola. When we were not at the station, she panicked thinking that we might have fallen asleep on the train and continued on towards Pensacola with it. She was greatly relieved when she later reached us by phone and learned that we were safely home. It's really kind of nice when your kids worry about you after all those years of worrying about them.

Returning to Mobile at the end of that trip, we still had a couple of vacation days left so we drove to Natchez, Mississippi and toured some of the Antebellum mansions there before returning to work.

We had another great vacation in February of 2000. It was a train trip from Mobile to Miami, Florida, with a one day layover in Orlando. On arriving in Miami, we rented a car and drove to Key West. We loved the Keys. It is such a warm, relaxing atmosphere that you just can't help feeling the stress melt away and having a great time. One memorable day at a sidewalk café in Key

West, we had a lunch of catfish sandwiches with sweet potato fries and a slice of key lime pie and all was well with the world. At that point we really felt that the layoff at Phillips was the best thing that ever happened to us.

If I had not been laid off but stayed with Phillips till retirement, we would have been much better off in some ways. The five weeks of vacation time each year and all the other benefits were really great, and the money was good too. On the other hand, however, we would have missed out on so much that we really enjoyed during those years of living in different places and seeing so many new things. We took a lot of pictures and filled a lot of albums with precious memories of good times in great places. A lot of those pictures included family members that were visiting and enjoying the sights with us. The so called good life with Phillips in Bartlesville was really getting to be boring after twenty-five years, and I really had all the winter weather I would ever need. I didn't care if I never saw another snowflake the rest of my life. So, all things considered, we both felt like our new life had become a series of adventures that gave us more joy than staying with Phillips ever could have.

In June of 2000, the great aircraft carrier The USS Enterprise docked for a few days at the Naval Air Station in Pensacola. We stood in line out in the heat for more than two hours to tour the ship, and it was well worth it. It was an amazing thing to see.

Randy, Angla, and Shelby were back for another visit over the fourth of July in 2000. We rented a pontoon boat and toured from Perdito Key to the Gulf at Ft. McRee, taking time to swim and see the dolphins along the way. Later in that month, John, Elese, and Brooke came to see us, and we took them on a tour boat down the same waterway to old Ft. McRee. Bill and Elaine came on July 25 and we went on the same tour boat with them and also toured an alligator farm. These times we got to be with family really helped to make living so far away more tolerable.

I think I should explain that running a large storage property involves much more than most folks realize. Both husband and wife must be able to handle all aspects of the office work including a great deal of computer operations. They must handle cash and credit card payments, fax machines, copiers, electronic gate systems, multiple phone lines, customer billings, vendor invoices, newspaper ads for auctions, reports for the home office, and a seemingly endless variety of things that are required to keep the office running smoothly. They must also be knowledgeable about a number of legal issues in order to protect the company from liability. In addition, the man must handle a wide variety of maintenance functions such as cleaning units, changing light bulbs all over the property, keeping driveways and common areas free of trash and debris, cutting locks, taking inventory of units up for auction, and doing minor repairs. I won't even try to describe the amount and types of trash and debris that customers will leave in units they vacate and all over the property. I'll just say that the man has to work very hard to take care of the property. It is certainly not the semi-retired kind of easy job many seem to think it is. Both members of the team must also be customer relations and sales experts. After all those years behind a desk in a corporate office, dealing with the public was a real education. This work involved a number of skills, but that was okay because we liked the variety and the independence the job gave us.

The storage business had been really good to us for the most part. It provided a steady income flow with housing provided and enabled us to go places and see things that we never could have experienced otherwise. This property was better built and designed than the others we had managed. There was a good customer base with a lot of long-term folks who became as much friends as customers. Our immediate boss was a regional manager with whom we got along very well. He would take us out to dinner and sometimes a movie whenever he was in town, and he was a buffer between us and the owner, giving us advice on how to keep the people at the top happy. We stayed with this job for four years, which was longer than anywhere else since the layoff at Phillips.

There were also, however, some negative aspects to this job as there always is. The worst was the work schedule. It was six days a week, with only Sunday off and very few holidays or other times to be away from the job. Next to that was the fact that this job also included renting U-Haul trucks in addition to managing the storage property. This was something we were not very well equipped to do, and we hated it. However, in our struggle for gainful employment through these years, we had learned to take the good with the bad and be grateful that our needs were being met. It was that attitude that enabled us to keep this job for four years.

However, by November of 2000 things were reaching the point where another change was needed. The boss we liked so much had left the company, and we were getting really frustrated with the six-day schedule and the trucks. The company offered us jobs as relief managers working out of the Houston area in a big RV, but we did not want that. We had been looking for opportunities with other companies nearby for quite some time with no success. The good thing that also made this difficult at the time was the fact that we were making more money than the other companies in our area were paying. We just had to face the fact that a move to another part of the country would be necessary.

One thing that made this more palatable was the fact that our daughter, Lori, was just finding out that her good job in Mobile was being transferred to a larger office in Memphis, Tennessee. Stu had found employment in Mobile and would have little trouble finding employment in Memphis. Since Lori and Stu would be moving to Memphis, the idea of our moving away from Mobile was made a lot easier.

ANOTHER MOVE—A NEW CHALLENGE

We interviewed with a company in the Dallas area and got an offer there, but it was far below the salary we were making in Mobile. Then we saw an opportunity far away near Harrisburg, Pennsylvania. It was far from family and the South we loved, but it was an opportunity to open and run a brand new property, and it offered the same level of pay we had been making. The owner flew us up there for an interview and made a good offer that involved a five-day week instead of six, so we took it. We moved into this strange new environment in November of 2000.

The property wasn't even finished yet, and the last building to be completed was the one containing the office and the apartment. The owner rented a townhouse nearby for us to live in until the apartment could be finished, and we worked out of it. We had a computer shipped to us, and I had to put it together in the townhouse and review a few different software programs that were designed for the storage business and pick one. I made my choice and began getting acquainted with how it worked. We shopped for furniture and equipment for the office, visited our competition, did some marketing, and with clipboard in hand, began renting units out in the driveway in the cold, while the workers finished building the counter and cabinets and other things to complete the office.

When the sawdust had been cleaned up and the builders were through in the office and apartment, we moved our furniture into the apartment from the storage units we had put it in and moved out of the townhouse. We also went with our boss to pick out furniture and decorations for the office and installed all the equipment such as copy and fax machines, telephones, and the computer. We hired a relief manager to work our days off and began our new life in another new place.

Fortunately, we were able to find a great new church home nearby in the town of Camp Hill. The congregation there welcomed us warmly, and we still stay in touch with one couple from there to this day.

Since we had never been in this part of the country, there was a wealth of new sights to see, and we did our best to make the most of the opportunity. At the risk of appearing totally insane, I'll describe our craziest adventure. This occurred on New Years Eve of 2000. Carole discovered a bus tour that would take us from our town, Mechanicsburg, to New York City arriving near Times Square at around 5:30 in the evening. We would be able to have dinner in the city, watch the ball drop at midnight, and get back on the bus at about 2:00 a.m. for the return trip. The best part was that I would not have to drive and park in New York City.

Knowing it would be cold, we layered up with lots of clothes but failed to take care of one critical element. In addition to the two pairs of socks, we should have worn rubber boots. The snow on the streets had turned to slush, and our feet eventually got very wet and cold. We were just fine from the ankle up, but when your feet are freezing, you are going to be miserable. We made it through the night, fortunately without getting frostbite.

We had a dinner reservation at an off-Broadway restaurant for 8:30 p.m. Since we wanted to see all we could between 5:30 and dinner time at 8:30, we started walking. Starting at Eighth Avenue and Fortieth Street we headed south as far as Fifth Avenue and Thirty-fourth Street. In that area we could see Macy's department store, Herald Square, and the Empire State building. The Empire State Building wasn't open at the time, so we could only see the outside of it. From there we went north up Fifth Avenue all the way to Central Park at Fifty-ninth Street. Along the way, we saw St. Patrick's Cathedral, Trump Tower (which was open and really beautiful), Sac's Fifth Avenue, and Rockefeller Center.

We had our picture taken in front of the Christmas tree at Rockefeller Center and watched the people ice skating for a while. Then we walked on to Central Park at Fifty-ninth Street over to Eighth Avenue and back south to our restaurant which was between Eighth and Ninth Avenues on Forty-sixth Street. If you are counting the blocks as you read along, you can see that we covered a lot of territory.

At about 9:30, after dinner, we went to get a spot on Seventh Avenue to watch the ball drop. Little did we know that to get a spot anywhere near Times Square (which is at Forty-third Street) you would have to get out there around noon and not move one inch until midnight. We later heard that some people wear adult diapers so they can hold on to their spot on the street. All of the stores and restaurants in the area had signs saying that their bathrooms were for customers only, but we managed to slip into a few of them. By the time we started looking for a place on the street, the police had barricaded off each block as it filled up with millions of people and the closest we could get was way back at Fifty-seventh Street, nearly back to Central Park. That is about fourteen blocks from Times Square and the ball looked pretty small from that distance, but at least we could see it. This was one of those things in life that you are glad you did once, but you would never do again. I really enjoy watching that ball drop on television from the comfort of my living room.

From November 2000 to June 2001, it was a cold, dreary climate, but we immersed ourselves in work and church and seeing all we could on our days off. There were many fascinating places to visit in one or two day trips from our new home near Harrisburg. In February of 2001, we made our first visit to Washington D.C. It was amazing! Tours inside the White House were closed on Sundays and Mondays, so we just walked all around the outside of the White House and the Old Executive Office Building next door. There was never enough time to really take everything in like we wanted to, but we made quick stops at the White House Visitors Center, some of the Smithsonian Museums, the Lincoln and Jefferson monuments, the Vietnam Memorial Wall, the Korean Memorial, the U.S. Capitol, and Arlington Cemetery.

The Washington Monument was closed for interior renovation so we could only see the outside of it. We were surprised to find that possibly the most beautiful building of all is the Library of Congress. When in Washington, don't miss it. In Arlington, we saw the famous Iwo Jima Memorial with five marines and one sailor raising the American flag.

At Arlington Cemetery, we saw John F. Kennedy's gravesite with the eternal flame, and the changing of the guard at the Tomb of the Unknown Soldier. This is a most impressive ceremony that is very moving to witness.

On February 12, we were on hand for the grand opening of The National Civil War Museum in Reservoir Park in Harrisburg. Governor Tom Ridge was the main speaker.

February 26 found us on a bus trip to Atlantic City, New Jersey. Soon after that we made our way to Hershey, Pennsylvania (just one of many trips to follow for that wonderful chocolate) and to Amish country near Lancaster, Pennsylvania. Another place we would return to often was Gettysburg with its Civil War battlefields, cemetery, and Lincoln history and statues. Next to Gettysburg, we visited Eisenhower's Farm. It was where he retired after serving as President.

Our wedding anniversary is March 13, and around that time we made a trip to Niagara Falls, spending a couple of nights at a quaint lodge on the Canadian side. Now, we enjoyed the trip, but I wouldn't say that March is the best time to go there. There was ice and snow everywhere and we could only be outside for short intervals because it was so miserably cold. Our oasis there was a beautiful Butterfly Conservatory that was full of lush tropical plants and a constant temperature of eighty degrees.

On March 17, Randy, Angla, and Shelby flew into Baltimore airport where I picked them up for a week-long visit. We enjoyed taking them to Amish country for that good Amish food and a ride in a horse drawn buggy. We also toured Gettysburg and Washington D.C. with them. Shelby was about five years old at the time, and he especially enjoyed the dinosaurs at the Natural History Museum. He and I both also enjoyed the free chocolate bar samples at the end of the tour at Chocolate World in Hershey.

In April, 2001 Lori and Stu came for a visit. We took them to Amish country, Gettysburg, the Eisenhower Farm, and Washington D.C. Repeat visits to these places were just as enjoyable as the first visit. I'll never forget the special feeling I got while standing on the steps of the Lincoln Monument with Abe sitting in his chair behind me while I gazed out over the reflecting pool to the Washington Monument in the distance. This is a really special place. It was on this visit to D.C. that we were lucky enough to get on a tour of the White House. Of course, the tour was very limited, but we did see the East Room where so many functions are held and several other rooms, all very impressive. We also took Lori and Stu to Arlington Cemetery where they got to see the changing of the guard, the Kennedy gravesite, and the mansion that once belonged to Robert E. Lee.

Later in April, Carole and I did some sightseeing at Valley Forge and Philadelphia. We saw Independence Hall and the Liberty Bell and just soaked up the history of it all. Getting to see all of these great places was wonderful and the job was going pretty well. There was, however, one problem. As much as we enjoyed visiting this part of the country, we really did not want to live there. Having endured one winter with all the cold dreary days and snow, we just did not want to face another one. You guessed it, we were about to move again.

TOO COLD— HEAD SOUTH

Having been at this job in Har-risburg for only seven months, we found a job with a company called Storage Spot in Orlando, Florida. We would have preferred a location closer to family, but this was all we could find at the time in a warm climate. It was a one-year old property with 730 units, and we moved there in June of 2001. We would stay there for two years.

This was a very nice property with both non-climate and climate-controlled units and the largest manager apartment we would have in all of the properties we ever managed. There was a relief manager to cover our days off, the company treated us well, and we were back in the warm Florida climate that we loved. It was a long way from family back home in Oklahoma and Kansas, but it was a wonderful place for them to come to see us. For people who love to get out and see things, this location was hard to beat. We had Disney World for starters and a long list of other attractions to enjoy with visitors or just on our own.

If it seems like Carole and I sure got around a lot for working folks, I might explain something here. When you live above or behind the office and you spend five days a week at that location, you really don't want to stay home on your days off. You feel like you just have to get out and go somewhere to get away from the work place and experience some rejuvenation. So that's what we did every chance we got.

The job went very well for the most part. There were no trucks to rent, and our area manager was a good guy to have for a boss. He came around a couple of times a month mostly for the work associated with auctions. The big bosses from the home office also treated us well, and our relief manager was dependable, so life in Orlando was good.

Lori and Stu came for visits in July and again at Thanksgiving. In October we met up with our friends from the church in Pennsylvania at their timeshare Condo in Daytona Beach. In September we went out to Ruidoso, New Mexico for a visit with Carole's brother, John, and his wife, Joyce.

At Christmas time that year, Carole and I went to Oklahoma for Christmas at our son Randy's house. That trip also included visits in Kansas with my dad and older brother, Gary, as well as Carole's brother, Bill, and his family.

Randy, Angla, and Shelby came down in March of 2002. We spent one day with them at Cocoa Beach over on the Atlantic side and three days at Disney World. We had one day at the Magic Kingdom, one day at Animal Kingdom, and one day at Epcot. We also spent one day with them at Universal Studios.

While living in Orlando we had season passes to all of the Disney parks and also to Sea World, which we enjoyed just as much and visited often. The great thing about that was how we could go to a park for just a few hours if we wished without rushing to do it all in one day. Even the parking was covered, so we would sometimes just go to Epcot, visit the French Pavillion for some of their great pastries, look around for a short time, and then leave.

In addition to seeing all the attractions in Orlando, we would also take one or two day trips to see other places all over the state. The church we settled into was a larger congregation than most of the others, but the folks were friendly and the sermons scriptural, so we liked it. The job was good, we were back in the state and the climate that we loved so much, and life was good. Once again we could say that the layoff at Phillips had just sent us on to a much richer and fuller life. That might sound like a strange thing to say after the trauma of the layoff and all the bumps in the road that led us over time to this place. The last job had only lasted seven months, and there were plenty of downsides to all the others along the way. The secret to finding joy in this journey was putting it all in perspective and realizing that the good things far outweighed the bad.

We were making many new friends and Christian brothers and sisters as we moved from place to place. If you are not part of a church family, you probably don't understand how close that relationship can be. Have you ever been told by people that are not related to you that they love you? When you miss a service you appreciate being told that you were missed and knowing that the one saying that really means it and wants to offer any help that might be needed.

In addition to all the good people we met along the way, we really enjoyed the experiences of living in different parts of the country. Even in the cold northern climate of Pennsylvania, we thoroughly enjoyed the times we spent seeing the sights in an area that we had never before visited. Now with this latest move we were back in the state we had always wanted to live in and working at the best job we had found since we got into the storage business.

In April of 2002 we visited Lori and Stu in Memphis. Their new home was actually a short drive from Memphis in Southaven, Mississippi. For the fourth of July that year, we were back at Southaven along with Randy and Shelby, who were there at the same time.

On the 26th of May we departed from Miami on our first Caribbean Cruise. It was a seven day cruise on Carnival Cruise Line's only totally non-smoking ship, the Paradise. We had a great time with stops in Nassau, San Juan, and St. Thomas on the eastern side of the Caribbean. There was a great variety of activities to choose from at each port, but we spent most of our land time touring each place to see as much of them as possible in the short time allowed. In Nassau we saw an old prison and a large straw market. In San Juan we toured an old fort called "Castillo de San Cristobal," then took a bus tour out through Puerto Rico's rain forest which was very beautiful. A highlight of the St. Thomas stop was the tram ride up to "Paradise Point," a hilltop view of the town and the harbor. Of course, all stops included shopping in an endless variety of souvenir stores.

Toward the end of July, Lori and Stu came to see us in Orlando. We took them over to Clearwater Beach for a luncheon cruise down the Intracoastal Waterway on a paddle boat. This was a favorite activity that we did with visitors several times. We also took them to Epcot. For a special dinner treat, we took them to High Tide Harry's, which was one of our all-time favorite seafood restaurants. For Labor Day in 2002, we spent the weekend down at Port Charlotte and Punta Gorda, Florida.

Carole's birthday is September 16th. On the 13th that year, she received a birthday card from my brother, Gary, with a short letter enclosed. It would be the last one, because he died the next day at the age of sixty-four. Of course, we joined the rest of the family in Independence, Kansas, for the funeral.

Back to work and life again in October, we would revisit the Disney parks and take in Cypress Gardens at Winter Haven, Florida. It is hard to describe the beauty of such places and how much they relieve stress and help in one's appreciation of life. Veteran's Day in November found us enjoying the sights and shows at Sea World in Orlando. On November 22 we went to see the Christmas light display at Disney's

MGM Studios. With five million lights, it was the biggest display we had ever seen.

For Christmas in '02 we went to Randy and Angla's house in Cushing, Oklahoma, and were joined by Bill and Elaine, as well as Lori, who was pregnant at the time. We also spent time at Bill and Elaine's house in Kansas with John, Elese, and Brooke.

In January of 2003 we went to one of our favorite places in Florida and that is John's Pass. It is a quaint little fishing village / tourist stop on the island south of Madeira Beach not far from the mouth of Tampa Bay. It boasts a boardwalk where tourists meet Pelicans, a fairly large number of shops, a marina where boats and jet skis can be rented, and another of our all-time favorite seafood restaurants called The Friendly Fisherman. In February we visited Lori and Stu at their home in Southaven near Memphis. If you are ever in Memphis, I suggest you eat at one of our all-time favorite barbeque restaurants, Corky's. Does it seem like I think about food a lot?

In March we visited the Kennedy Space Center and really enjoyed that. During that month we also went to Homosassa Springs State Wildlife Park. That is a truly beautiful place where you can see alligators, manatees, herons, pelicans, and a number of other examples of exotic wildlife. The following day we went to Weeki-Wachee Springs, which boasts much of the same wildlife and scenery. The natural springs feed into a river, and on the boat ride down the river, several pelicans landed with a thud on the canvas top of our tour boat to get the fish our driver would toss to them. There was also a very large glass sided tank where "mermaids" would perform their underwater ballet.

Another attraction in that part of Florida that we enjoyed more than once is Tarpon Springs. It is a Greek fishing village with a long history of sponge diving. You can eat Greek food and learn everything you ever wanted to know about sponges - the real ones.

On April 17, 2003 our daughter Lori gave birth to our second grandson, Jordan. This happened in Southaven, Mississippi, and we drove straight through from Orlando, but did not make it in time for the blessed event. Our first grandson, Shelby, was about seven at the time, and we now had one grandson from our son and one from our daughter. We are blessed to have two wonderful grandsons.

The month of May found us traveling to Silver Springs, Florida, and to St. Petersburg for the Pier and the Sunken Gardens. Later that month, around Memorial Day, we went to St. Augustine which is another of our favorite places in Florida. It has a lighthouse which we just have to climb whenever we are there. It also has an old fort and a number of historic sites. We enjoyed a restaurant there called the Santa Maria which is on a pier out over the water. It has little doors in the wall next to the tables through which the diners can throw bread to the fish. There I go talking about eating places again. In June we went to see South Beach in Miami. It was just one more place to check off our list.

FAMILY CALLS

We had now been in Orlando for two years, and as much as we loved it there, we were really beginning to feel too far removed from our family back in Oklahoma and Kansas.

Our daughter had given us this new grandson we longed to spoil, and we also missed Shelby and the rest of the family. By this time Lori, Stu, and Jordan had moved from Southaven, Mississippi to Cushing, Oklahoma, which is where Randy and his family lived.

Storage Spot had been good to us so the job was not a problem, but the desire to be closer to our family was just too strong to stay there. The company had properties in the Dallas/Fort Worth area but no manager vacancies at the ones we would have liked at the time. Their property in Grand Prairie, Texas was the one we thought we would really like, but it was not available then. We did not know it at the time, but we would end up there at a later date.

Finding a similar job at a decent storage property in Oklahoma was not easy. The owners in Oklahoma did not pay as well as those in Florida or Texas, and openings were few and far between. Finally, we landed a job with a company in Oklahoma City which would put us just a little over an hour from Cushing and both of our kids and their families. This was the first time we ever took a job without ever seeing the property, but it was a gamble we thought was worth taking.

We would make the move and start this new job in July of 2003. Around the middle of June we said goodbye to the Florida beaches we loved with a trip over to Sand Key State Park just south of Clearwater Beach. We had a picnic at a table under some trees near the water's edge and then spent the afternoon reading and relaxing in our beach chairs. We just enjoyed watching the boats come in and out from the Bay to the Gulf and took in the scenery while the Pelicans flew by. We had one of the most relaxing days ever. It was sad to think of leaving this beautiful place, but our family meant more to us than anything, and we really wanted to be close enough to see them often.

Our family all came to help us get moved in. They cleaned the place we would live in, which was a mess, brought food, and helped us tremendously. The property turned out to be a disaster in many ways, but we thought being this close to our family made it all worthwhile.

This was a very large property with 799 units including 150 outside RV spaces. All of the buildings except one were very old and had been poorly maintained. All of the RV spaces were on dirt or gravel surface, and what little paving had been done was in poor shape. The owners had refused to spend the money necessary to put the property in good condition, and that applied to the manager residence as well. The office and living quarters were in an old house that had been converted for this use.

Rather than replace the worn carpet in the living space, the owner took it all out and put in cheap vinyl tile. There was a basement, and when it rained, you could hear water gushing into it and reaching a level of about four feet in depth. This was right in the middle of "tornado alley," and this basement offered no safety at all, not to mention the rats, mold, and other possible horrors that inhabited it. When customers complained about the huge ruts in the driveways, we were told to try to get them to pay for the repairs. We could not believe that the owner actually expected customers to pay for repairs to his property. To top it all off, we also had to rent trucks.

In spite of the fact that this was the worst property we had ever run, we were glad to be so close to our family. We enjoyed being able to be with them often and just made the best of a bad situation at work.

It wasn't long, however, before we were searching all over the area for a better storage company to work for. We soon discovered that nicer properties were available but they did not offer the pay we were getting and in most cases, did not offer any health insurance, which we considered essential. In addition, many companies were offering full-time employment to the wife only with the husband getting to work only about twenty hours per week. Eventually we realized that to stay in Oklahoma, we would pretty well be stuck where we were. We just did the best we could with the job situation while keeping our eyes open for any other opportunities. We stayed in touch with Storage Spot thinking that the Grand Prairie property might eventually be our best option.

The only bright spot in this situation was the opportunity it provided for being with our family so much more than had been possible up to this time. For Thanksgiving in 2003 we hosted the dinner for our kids and their families, Bill, Elaine, John, Elese and Brooke, Elaine's brother, Charles, and Lori's in-laws who lived in Stillwater. There were fourteen guests in all, and we had a great time. At Christmas that year, we spent time at Randy and Angla's house in Cushing and at Bill and Elaine's place near Independence, Kansas. The celebration at Bill and Elaine's also included my dad, who was eighty-nine years old at the time.

In February, we helped Bill and Elaine celebrate their fortieth wedding anniversary with many of their friends and family, and it was great to be so close to everyone that we could share so many good times together.

As much as we enjoyed this closeness with so much of our family, however, the job was still very difficult to deal with, and in March, Storage Spot offered us the chance to manage their nice property in Grand Prairie, Texas. It would just be about a five-hour drive from Cushing, and we were glad that we had not burned any bridges. We had only been in Oklahoma City for about eight months, and now we were making another move, this time back to Texas.

HEADING SOUTH AGAIN

After having stayed with one job for twenty five years before being laid off, we were sure making a lot of moves and a lot of job changes during these next twelve years. That seemed to be necessary as we struggled to balance family ties and job satisfaction with results that seemed to be only temporary at best.

We made it back to Cushing for Jordan's first birthday party in April and made that trip often as we tried to see our family as much as possible. When any of our family came to see us, we took them to Texas Ranger baseball games, the Six Flags Amusement Park, and lots of other places around the Dallas / Fort Worth area.

By the time my dad's ninetieth birthday rolled around in July of 2004, he was living at an assisted-living facility in Independence, Kansas. We were there, along with my sister and her husband from Denver and most of the rest of our family, for a big birthday party my sister had arranged for him.

This job at Grand Prairie, back with Storage Spot, who had employed us in Orlando for two years, did not turn out as well as expected. There was a problem with the company apartment located above the office that prevented us from moving into it, so we had to put our furniture in storage units. The company put us up in an apartment near the storage property, and we began our work there while waiting for the company apartment to become available so we could move our stuff once again.

As if that wasn't bad enough, we had no relief manager. The way we got our two days off was that

I would have to go run the property in Arlington for two days giving those managers their days off and leaving my wife to run our property alone for those two days. Then the Arlington manager would come to our place for two days leaving his wife alone at their property so we could have our days off. The company only had one property in Orlando, so this had not been an issue there, but it was a real problem here. I even had to go way over to east Dallas once in a while to fill in for the manager at the company's huge property over there.

To top it all off, in August we found out that Storage Spot, the whole company - some twenty-two properties in several states, was being bought out by another storage company. We really started to worry as time passed and we were getting no information from either side as to how this would affect us. We did not know if the new company would want to keep us or bring in other people. When you remember that, in this business, if you lose your job, you lose your home as well, you can see why we began to get a little nervous.

THE BEST IS LAST

With all this in mind, we once again found ourselves looking for another company to work for. Finally, this time we hit the jackpot. A company called Lock-N-Key Storage needed managers for a property they had over in east Dallas, close to Mesquite, Texas. In September of 2004, we started work for them and they turned out to be the best company we had ever worked for. As time passed, we could not believe how great these people were and how much better they treated all their employees than anyone else we had ever seen. They were always ready to authorize whatever spending was necessary to keep the property in good shape and often surprised us with extra rewards for any extra effort or accomplishment.

One thing that is rather unique to the storage business is how the manager's pay package is structured. All of these companies pay their managers with a combination of salary and bonus money. They base their bonus plans on a variety of factors, including such things as occupancy percentage, revenue goals, success in collection of delinquent payments, and sale of boxes, locks, and miscellaneous items. The plans vary greatly among the different companies, and the bonus portion is often a very significant part of the total pay package. That meant that if a manager couple did not do well at meeting bonus goals, their income suffered.

The bad thing about being so dependent on the bonuses is the fact that it is impossible to fashion a plan that is fair to managers throughout the company. Many factors such as the location of the property (rich neighborhood or poor one), local economic trends, and other factors make it much easier for managers in some locations to meet bonus goals than for those in other places to meet the same goals.

We were fortunate to find that Lock-N-Key's bonus plan allowed for our income at the Dallas property to be fairly consistent and generous. We worked there for three and one-half years which turned out to be the best years of our career in storage.

This company was so outstanding that they did something totally unheard of in this industry. About every eighteen months they would fly in manager couples from their properties all over the country to some beautiful resort hotel for a seminar that would include two days for travel and two or three days for meetings and fun. We got in on two of those. The first one was at a beautiful resort near San Antonio and the second was at a fabulous hotel in Vail, Colorado.

Another feature of this company made it stand out from all the rest. While some other storage companies hired manager couples to run their properties, they only used individuals to serve as relief managers to cover the property when the regular managers were off. Lock-N-Key was the only company we ever saw that hired couples to fill the relief manager positions. This was a great thing because it is very difficult for one person to handle it all alone. The work requires someone to be in the office and someone outside on the property showing units, cleaning units, and doing various other things. It is a little hard for one person to be two places at the same time, so something has to give. That means missed phone calls and visits from potential customers. This company really knew how to handle the business and keep good managers happy. As a result, they had far less manager turnover than other storage companies.

Another good thing about this job was that we found a very good church just a short distance from the property where there were good elders, good preachers, and friendly people. Finding good churches in so many different places around the country is quite remarkable when you realize that Churches of Christ are totally autonomous. There is no hierarchy such as state, regional, or national organizations. Each and every congregation is totally independent and the only thing keeping them together is the Bible. There is no creed book of any kind. That means that when people in different places just honestly try to follow the Bible, they are able to do just that. They come up with the same teaching and the same type of worship. You have probably heard it said that different people interpret the Bible differently, but that is just a cop-out that does not have to be true when people will honestly accept what the Bible clearly says without trying to put their own ideas into it. We proved that in Alabama, Pennsylvania, Florida, Oklahoma, and Texas. I even found it in Lagos, Nigeria.

So the job was good, the church was good, and we were close enough to family to see them fairly often. When Thanksgiving Day came in 2004, we had most of the Kansas and Oklahoma family packed into our fairly small apartment in Dallas. Several times while there, we put people on air mattresses on the floor and wherever we could so that we could all be together. In December that year, Carole's brother, John, and his wife, Joyce, moved from Ruidoso, New Mexico to

Leander, Texas, which is just at the north side of Austin.

In February of 2005, Lori, Stu, and Jordan, who would be two in April, came to see us. We treated them to a lunch at the revolving restaurant atop the Reunion Tower, which was something we did with just about everyone who came to see us in Dallas. It was President's Day, and there was a real secret service agent in the restaurant giving a talk during the lunch time.

In March, we took our second Caribbean Cruise. This time we departed from Galveston and toured the western side of the Caribbean on another Carnival ship, the Elation. Port stops around the Yucatan Peninsula included Progreso, Cozumel, and Belize. Points of interest at Progreso included Colonial Izamal, which was a Spanish colonial city founded in the fifth century A.D.

After docking at the island of Cozumel, we took a smaller boat to Playa Del Carmen on the mainland. There we boarded a bus for the trip to the Mayan Ruins at Tulum. These ruins sit on a bluff overlooking a sandy beach at the edge of the Caribbean. There is tropical foliage all around and Palm trees and the water is clean and clear and it is one of the most beautiful places I have ever seen. After the boat ride back to Cozumel, we had a little over an hour before we had to be back on the ship, so we toured Cozumel in a horse drawn buggy and looked around some shops near the cruise ship.

The next stop was Belize City in the country of Belize, which is on the Yucatan coast next to Guatemala. The water at the shoreline was too shallow for the docking of cruise ships, so the ship dropped anchor some distance from the shore, and we were taken in on smaller boats called tenders. At Belize City we took a tour on a bus that included a ride out to the Mayan Ruins at Altun Ha. There the steps up the sides of one of the temples were in good enough condition that we were allowed to climb up to the top and view the whole area from that vantage point. Back in Belize City, we enjoyed a lunch of coconut shrimp and did some shopping before going back to the ship.

Then we headed back to Galveston and back to work in Dallas. As much as we enjoyed our two cruises, and we really did have a great time, we are not sure we want to do another one. The reason is the short amount of time you are given at each port before you have to be back on board for the next leg of the trip. We always felt like we would have really liked to have more time to spend at each place.

In April, we helped celebrate Jordan's second birthday at a Mexican restaurant in Tulsa, Oklahoma and attended our first company seminar at the Hyatt Hill Country Resort in San Antonio. At the end of May, we spent three days in Galveston, a place we would enjoy visiting a few more times during our time in Dallas.

In July of 2005, we went to Crawford, Texas, where President George W. Bush has a ranch nearby. It was another place where we would visit more than once and bring relatives on some trips. The little town has a restaurant and gas station that is a good place to eat. There are Bush photos all over the walls. There are also a few souvenir shops with all kinds of Bush souvenirs, T-shirts, posters, and cowboy hats. The drive past the Bush ranch about eight miles from town is fun, but all you can see from the road is the gate and a building that houses some secret service people.

There are signs all over the place telling you not to stop, but just keep on going. You definitely get the feeling that they are not kidding, and I was not about to test them.

Also in July, we got a visit from Bill and Elaine and Brooke, and Carole's other brother, John, and his wife, Joyce. It was fun having that bunch all together. We took them all to lunch at the revolving restaurant atop the Reunion Tower in downtown Dallas.

In August, Lori and Jordan came to see us and brought Brooke along. We rode the trains from Dallas to Fort Worth and took them to the Fort Worth Zoo. We also got in a visit to Six Flags. Later in August, Randy, Angla, and Shelby came to Dallas, and we took them to Six Flags and the Fort Worth Zoo, also.

In September, we had a vacation planned for Mount Rushmore in South Dakota. We went through Cushing, Oklahoma and picked up Lori and Jordan who went on with us. One day on the trip, Jordan got really sick, but most of the time was very enjoyable for all of us, and after a visit to a local urgent care center and a dose of medicine, Jordan recovered pretty quickly. Even though he was only two years old, Jordan was soon saying the names of those four presidents. Other highlights of that trip included the 1880's train ride from Keystone, SD to Hill City, SD and a visit to Bear Country, USA which provided the chance to see lots and lots of bears of all ages and sizes up close.

In November, we were in Cushing to see all the family there and celebrate grandson Shelby's tenth birthday. We also made it up to Kansas to see Carole's brother, Bill, and his family. For Thanksgiving in 2005, we did something a little different. Carole's brother, John, and his wife, Joyce, were with us in Dallas and we wanted to be with all the Oklahoma and Kansas folks as well. So we all met at a restaurant in McAlester, Oklahoma, which was about half-way between us and them. There were sixteen of us in all. Christmas that year was at our apartment in Dallas with Carole's two brothers and their wives as well as John, Elese, and Brooke, and Elaine's brother, Charles. Our son and daughter were at Randy's house in Cushing with their families that year. Lori, Stu, and Jordan came to see us in Dallas in January 2006.

In March of 2006, we celebrated our fortieth wedding anniversary with a trip to Montego Bay, Jamaica. We were gone a week, with two days for flying there and back and five days enjoying the beauty of the island. Our hotel was right across from a beautiful beach, called Doctor's Cave Beach, with views of the Caribbean from several balconies. It was one of the best vacations we ever had. The atmosphere is very laid back, and the most commonly heard phrase is "No Problem, Mon." We spent a little time on the beach and went on various tours every day. One such tour took us through an eighteenth century mansion called Rose Hall where the infamous owner, Annee Palmer, is said to have murdered three husbands and a number of lovers. Another tour of a plantation area included breakfast and a roasted pig at a Jamaican buffet-luncheon on the porch of the pavilion house overlooking lush tropical foliage.

Another day's highlight was to the famous Dunn's River Falls where the water cascades six hundred feet over rocks descending nearly like stair steps to end at the beach at the beautiful Caribbean Sea. After walking down to the beach, you get in the water and walk and climb up over the rocks through the water to the top of the falls. I made it all the way to the top, but Carole gave it up and got out about three fourths of the way up.

We got to see crocodiles on a boat tour on the Black River and spent one day on a seven-mile stretch of white sand beach at a place called Negril. At the end of the day in Negril, we went to a place called Rick's Café for dinner and enter-tainment. The restaurant sits near the edge of some cliffs overlooking a cove on the Caribbean coastline. The entertainment included live music and boys and young men diving off the cliffs for tips. Guests were allowed to jump or dive from the cliffs also and some did, but we just watched. I guess you might call us cowards. As though the cliffs were not high enough, some of the divers would climb up to a perch at the top of a tree at the cliff's edge and dive off from there. Dinner was very good and as the sun set on the water to cap off the end of a perfect day, we boarded the bus for the ride back to our hotel.

In April of 2006, we were in Cushing for Jordan's first Easter egg hunt. He was two days short of being three years old. His birthday party was at his house in Cushing with most of the family and a number of friends present. I wore a tee shirt that said "Grandpa is my name, Spoilin' is my game."

May of 2006 brought a major event to our lives. We knew that we were planning to retire in about two more years and that we would live in Cushing because our kids and grandkids were there. What we did not expect, however, was that we would happen to find the perfect house at that time. The house had just been finished and was great, but what made it really special was its location. It sat on a three-acre lot just outside of town that was mostly trees and very secluded and peaceful. After more than thirteen years living in big, noisy, crowded cities, we knew we wanted to retire in a quiet place. The problem, of course, was that we were two years short of being ready to retire and move from Dallas to Cushing.

Fortunately for us, there was a solution for this problem. When I was abruptly forced to leave Phillips after a twenty-five year career there, I had some company stock that we put into a mutual fund account with a broker in Tampa, Florida.

Over the next thirteen years, it grew in value, so we had some savings there. In addition to that, there was some money inherited from my father when he died in 2004, so we were financially able to buy this house. We did not want it to just sit empty for two years, so we put in the rest of the appliances and window blinds and rented it to a doctor who had just come to town and did not know if he would be staying long enough to purchase a house for himself. As it turned out, he left after only about six months and we did not want to rent it again. We handled that by putting in just enough furniture so we could stay in it when we came to town instead of staying with our children. On many future trips, we enjoyed using it and slowly getting it ready for our final move, which would come on March 1, 2008.

It was amazing to think about how lucky we were to be in this position, with our retirement house already bought, after the terror of the layoffs in 1992 and the turbulent years that followed, going from one job to another to keep some kind of roof over our heads. I was reminded once again of what I said in the introduction about how no matter how tough things get, there will be better days ahead if you just don't give up, but keep on going. We had enjoyed many better days and happy times even in the midst of those many moves from place to place and job to job.

My sixty-second birthday rolled around in June of 2006, and our great-niece, Brooke, had spent a few days with us in Dallas. Her parents, John and Elese, and grandparents, Bill and Elaine, came down to pick her up and celebrate my birthday. The fourth of July that year found Carole and me in Branson, Missouri enjoying some music shows and a few days of rest and relaxation.

Later in July, our world would be turned upside down. Elaine, the wife of Carole's brother Bill, had been in rather poor health for quite some time with diabetes and other problems, but we were all totally unprepared for her death on July 18 at the age of fifty-nine. Bill and Elaine had been converted from a denomination years earlier and were faithful, hard-working members of the Church of Christ in Independence. When Elaine became ill on July 12, she was working in the kitchen at a church camp near Sedan, Kansas, cooking for all the kids. First, she was taken to the hospital in Sedan, then to Bartlesville, OK, and finally to St. John's Hospital in Tulsa, where she passed away on the eighteenth. It seemed all too soon, and we all still miss her very much, but we get comfort from knowing that she was a faithful Christian who is now in the hands of our loving God.

Later, Bill came to Dallas with us to spend some time with us there, as did Carole's other brother, John, with his wife Joyce. At Grapevine, Texas, on the northwest side of Dallas, there is a large resort hotel, the Gaylord Texan, and a converted military amphibious vehicle called a "Duck" that takes visitors on tours on both land and lake. We all had a good time on the "Duck." The driver even let Bill and John have a turn at driving the thing. We went out on it several other times when various family members came to see us. A few days later on that same visit, we took Bill to the famous Stockyards in Fort Worth, which was another of those places where we often went with visitors.

In August of 2006, we took a week's vacation to Corpus Christi, Texas and took our grandson Shelby along with us. We visited an aquarium and the aircraft carrier USS Lexington, which

Shelby said was his favorite part of the trip. We also went to the beach and met up with John and Joyce at Padre Island National Seashore, where we all enjoyed the sand and surf. We made time on the way home to Dallas to stop at San Antonio and take Shelby to the Alamo and the Tower of the Americas in Hemisfair Park. I thought the great Mexican dinner right beside the river walk was a highlight of that trip.

In September, we got to go to Lock-N-Key's manager's conference at a beautiful Resort Hotel and Spa in Vail, Colorado. This company really knew how to put on a meeting.

My sister, Linda and her husband, Don, came to see us in October of 2006, and we enjoyed having lunch with them at the revolving restaurant atop Reunion Tower in downtown Dallas. For Thanksgiving that year we had Bill and John and Joyce at our place in Dallas as well as John, Elese, and Brooke.

Our vacation in February of 2007 took us to Cancun, Mexico, one of those tourist hot-spots on the coast of the Yucatan Peninsula. We had cruised to this part of the world previously, but this time we flew in so we could spend most of a week in one area. We stayed at an all-inclusive beach-front resort and had a great time, but we are not sure we would do the all-inclusive thing again. All of the meals are covered in the package price, but we were out sightseeing a lot and having to buy meals in other places. We don't like to stay in one place long enough to get the full advantage of a package deal.

A highlight of this trip was the all-day bus tour to the Chichen Itza Mayan Ruins. The trip included lunch at a restaurant called Hacienda Xaybe'h, which featured young people dancing with dishes on their heads and a stop at a huge ancient well that you can actually go down into and swim—or not. Another day trip was to a gorgeous park called Xcaret. It is kind of a cross between a theme park and a zoological garden. A small river runs through it, and we were able to put on life jackets and just float down the river, enjoying the tropical beauty along the way. There was a wonderful buffet-lunch in a large pavilion right next to the sea and a dinner show in the evening in a large arena with lots of singers and dancers acting out various parts of Mexico's history while we ate our meal. Those two day trips were among the best we have ever had, anywhere.

When March of 2007 rolled around, we had Randy and Shelby down for a visit along with Brooke and her friend, Amy. We all had fun at a Dallas go-cart track and game place and also rode the Duck out at Grapevine Lake. In April it was Lori, Jordan, and Bill with us on the Duck with four-year-old Jordan doing part of the driving as the Captain's helper. Bill and Carole also got in the act.

During the month of May we had John and Elese and Carole's brother, John, with us to celebrate both Mother's Day and John and Elese's birthdays. They were both turning forty that year, her April 2, and him May 18. Brother John joined his wife, Joyce, at the home of some of her relatives in Fort Worth and we took John and Elese to the Dallas Arboretum, which boasts a large array of gardens in a beautiful setting on the shores of Whiterock Lake. We then joined up with John and Joyce at their home in Leander, Texas, near Austin along with John and Elese. Before returning north to Dallas, we took John and Elese to see the George H.W. Bush Presidential Library in College Station, Texas.

Stu, Lori, and Jordan came back to see us in June, around Lori's birthday, and we celebrated with them at Rockwall Harbor on the lake just east of Dallas, and with visits to the Dallas Arboretum, the Fort Worth Water Gardens and Stockyards, and the Dallas Aquarium. This aquarium in downtown Dallas is not many years old, and it is a very first-rate aquarium, well worth a visit. Lori and Jordan were back again in October, and this visit included a trip to the Fort Worth Zoo.

In September of 2007 we took the last vacation of our working lives which was a trip to Las Vegas. We had never been there before, and we just thought we should at least see it once. We really don't like casinos and neither smoke nor drink, but we had heard that there were lots of things to do and see there that we would enjoy, and we found that to be very true. Every hotel was practically a city in itself with each one having its own theme and something to see. There are the lions at MGM Grand, the dolphins and tigers at The Mirage, the Eiffel Tower and shops at The Paris Hotel, and the ride in a gondola at

The Venetian. Probably the most famous of all is the Bellagio with its fabulous fountains which are timed to music. The eye-popping sights and sounds were all around, and we only went to one show. That was a group of impersonators performing as such stars as Elvis, Michael Jackson, and others, and to my surprise, they were very, very good. Celine Dion was nearing the end of her run at Caesar's Palace, and we would have loved the chance to see her, but she was on a break from performing when we were there.

One day we took a bus tour out over Hoover Dam to the Grand Canyon, and that was an enjoyable trip, even though it involved many hours of riding on the bus. Still, walking along the canyon edge and taking pictures was lots of fun, and Hoover Dam was also a very impressive sight.

During the last few months of 2007 and the very first of 2008, John, Elese, and Brooke lived in our house in Cushing while they looked for a house to buy. Bill was already living in Cushing, along with Randy and Lori and their families. John had found a good job, and they wanted to be near family. As it turned out, they found their house and vacated ours shortly before we were ready to move into it.

Well, all this time at Lock-N-Key Storage, starting back in September of 2004, this job continued to be the best one we had ever had. We had run newer, nicer properties, but we had never worked for a company as good as this one. Of course, there were problems that cropped up once in a while as there is with any job, and particularly when you have to work directly with the public. But our superiors at the home office always backed us up and gave us whatever support was needed to handle whatever came along. They appreciated our efforts and let us know it, and we appreciated them.

I said before that even through some tough times after the layoff, I found myself in a place more than once when I could feel like my life was better after losing the job with Phillips than it would have been had I remained there to retirement. Carole also felt the same way, and we definitely felt it with this job in Dallas. I hope this will encourage anyone going through a layoff to see how our lives were improved by it. I also want to remind you that our faith and our church family played a big part in helping us through those tough days that came before things got better.

THE "R" WORD— RETIREMENT

Towards the end of 2007, we found ourselves facing two situations. One was trying to decide just when would be the best time for us to retire and move into our house in Cushing near our family. I was sixty-three years old, and I certainly did not want to work to age sixty-five. The other factor was that our company, Lock-N-Key Storage, was on the market. The owners had decided it might be a good time to sell. We certainly did not want to start over with another storage company, and we did not even know if the new owners would want to keep us anyway or pay as much as we were used to getting. Finally, we made the decision to retire at the end of February in 2008. That turned out to be a good choice, because the company did change hands shortly after that.

With the help of all our family, we moved into our house in Cushing on March 1, 2008, and began our new life in retirement. With forty-two years of work behind me, I was ready to enjoy the fruits of my labor and the blessings of God, who brought me safely through to this great new place. I don't know what troubles the future may bring, but I do know that I have been richly blessed to come this far and I am ready to trust that the days ahead will be all right too. Fortunately, this community has a great church family, and we love being a part of it. Needless to say, we also love being together with so much of our physical family. Now we have the grandkids sports activities, the birthdays and other holiday celebrations, and lots of wonderful times to be with the ones we love so much. To say that retirement beats holding down a job would be a great understatement.

After twenty-five-plus years with Phillips Petroleum Company, all in Bartlesville, Oklahoma, our job hunt involved moving thirteen times, in five states, with seven different companies, within a fifteen year period. Some would look at that and say that's terrible. Not us. We got to live places we never would have lived, see things we never would have seen, meet wonderful people we never would have met, learned things we never would have learned, and become part of church families with brothers and sisters in Christ in all of those places. We wouldn't trade that for anything.

Well that's my story, and I hope you are encouraged by it. If you have been laid off, just don't give up. No one losing a job could possibly feel more desperate than I felt. Keep on trying for that great new job. Keep a positive attitude, be flexible, try new things, and rest assured that there are better days in your future. The secret is in trusting that the best is yet to come. With God's help, it will be.